50 FILM TUNES FOR PIANO GRADED

Published by
Wise Publications
14-15 Berners Street, London W1T 3LJ, UK.

Exclusive Distributors:
Music Sales Limited
Distribution Centre, Newmarket Road,
Bury St Edmunds, Suffolk IP33 3YB, UK.
Music Sales Corporation
257 Park Avenue South, New York, NY 10010, USA.
Music Sales Pty Limited
20 Resolution Drive, Caringbah, NSW 2229, Australia.

Order No. AM998547
ISBN 978-1-84938-234-2
This book © Copyright 2009 Wise Publications,
a division of Music Sales Limited.

Edited by Jenni Wheeler.
Music processed by Camden Music.
Printed in the EU.

Your Guarantee of Quality
As publishers, we strive to produce every book to
the highest commercial standards.
This book has been carefully designed to minimise awkward
page turns and to make playing from it a real pleasure.
Particular care has been given to specifying acid-free, neutral-sized
paper made from pulps which have not been elemental chlorine bleached.
This pulp is from farmed sustainable forests and
was produced with special regard for the environment.
Throughout, the printing and binding have been planned to ensure
a sturdy, attractive publication which should give years of enjoyment.
If your copy fails to meet our high standards,
please inform us and we will gladly replace it.

www.musicsales.com

WISE PUBLICATIONS
part of The Music Sales Group

London / New York / Paris / Sydney / Copenhagen / Berlin / Madrid / Tokyo

GRADING NOTES

The pieces in this book have been carefully graded according to
various criteria such as rhythmic complexity, phrasing, tempo, key, range, etc.
Look for the number of stars for each piece to give you
an idea of the approximate playing level.
All musicians have particular strengths and weaknesses,
so the grading offered here should be taken as a suggestion only.

Generally, pieces with one star will have simple rhythms
in both hands and straight forward phrasings.
They are essentially diatonic and in easier keys.

Pieces with two stars will have more challenging passages,
perhaps containing more rhythmic complexity
and possibly explore a wider range on the keyboard.

Three-star pieces may be in more challenging keys
and include some modulation.
Read through rhythms and keys carefully before playing,
and check for time-signature changes.

All Love Can Be
(from 'A Beautiful Mind')

Words by Will Jennings & Music by James Horner

Moderately slow ♩ = 68

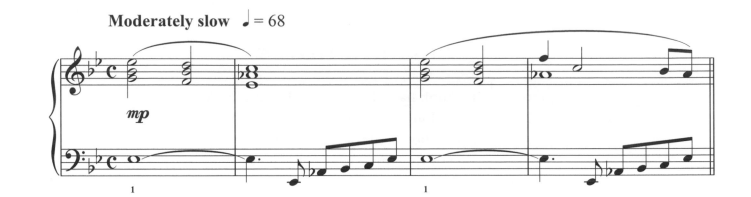

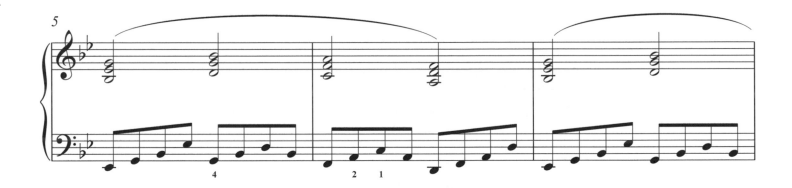

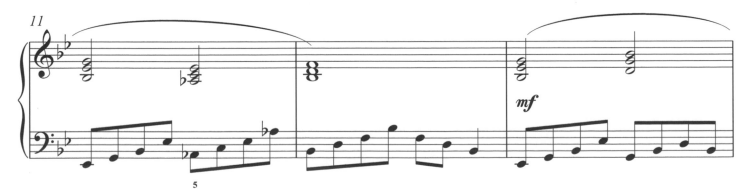

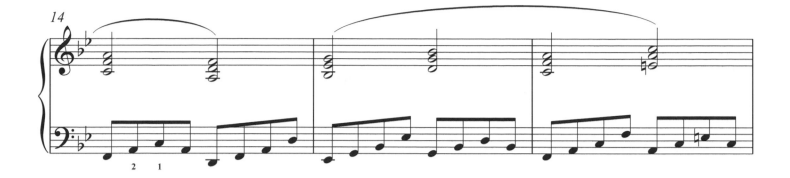

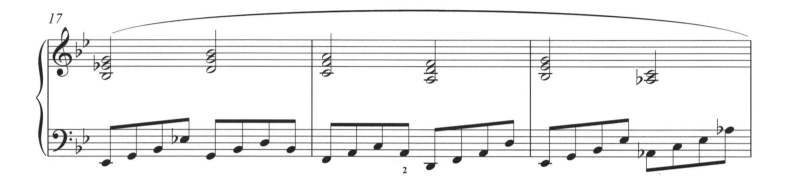

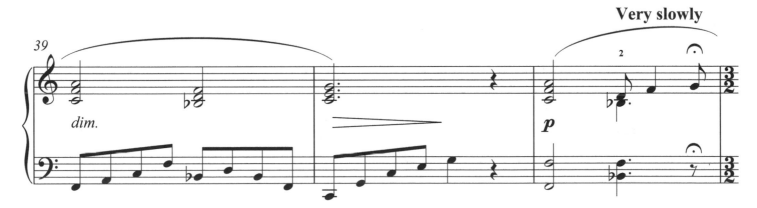

Down Over Lake Victoria
(from 'The Last King Of Scotland')

Music by Alex Heffes

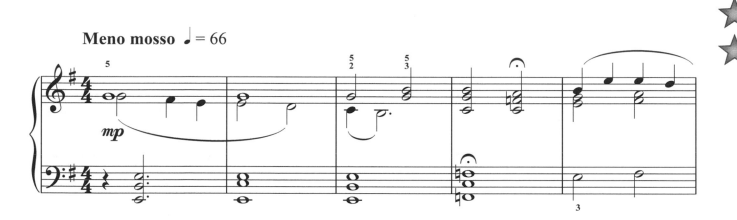

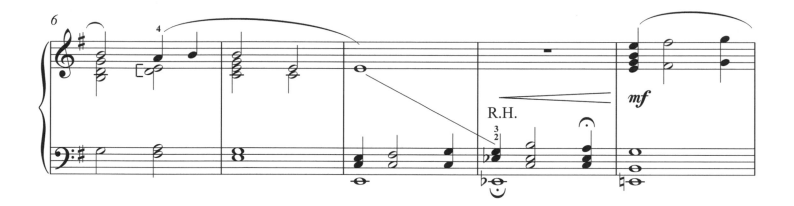

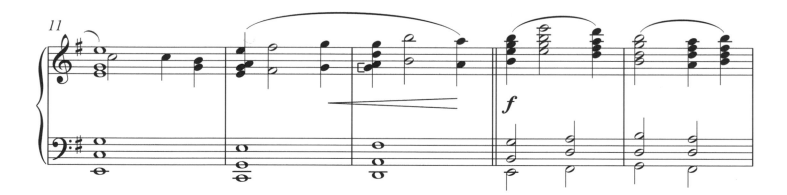

The Winner Is
(from 'Little Miss Sunshine')

Music by Mychael Danna, Thomas Hagerman, Nicholas Iurato, Shawn Gilbert & Jean Schroder

Moderately ♩ = 104

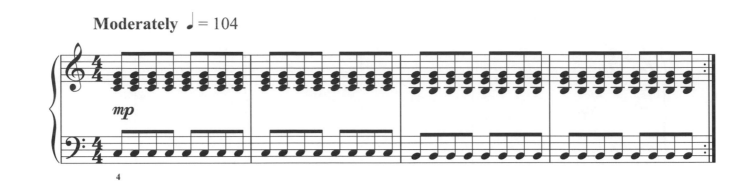

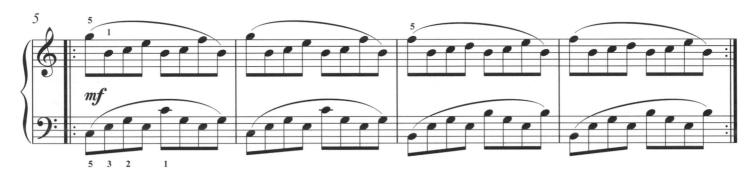

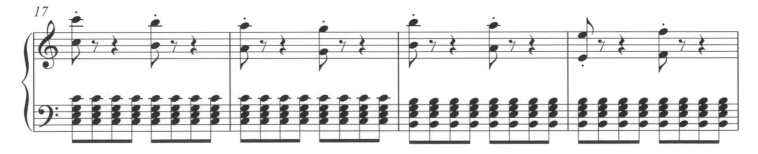

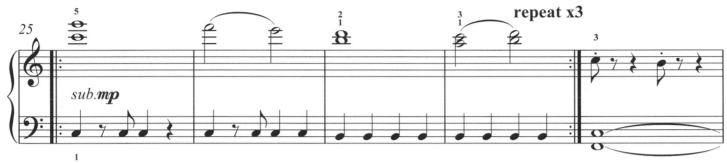

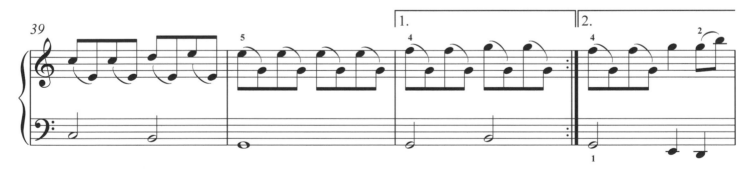

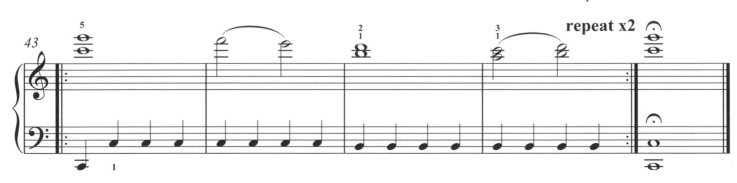

Aria from 'Goldberg Variations'
(from 'The English Patient')

Music by Johann Sebastian Bach

Execution of the ornaments

Steadily

Baby Elephant Walk
(from 'Hatari!')

Music by Henry Mancini

Moderately slow and steady

Very slowly

Back To The Future (Theme)
(from 'Back To The Future')

Music by Alan Silvestri

With movement

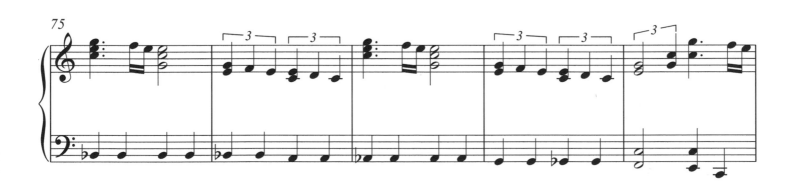

Betty et Zorg
(from 'Betty Blue')

Music by Gabriel Yared

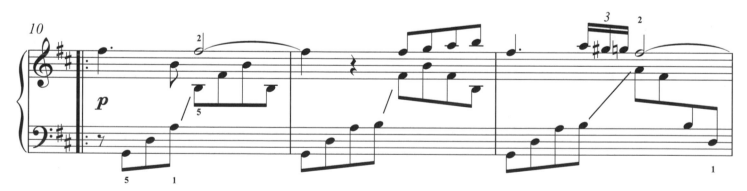

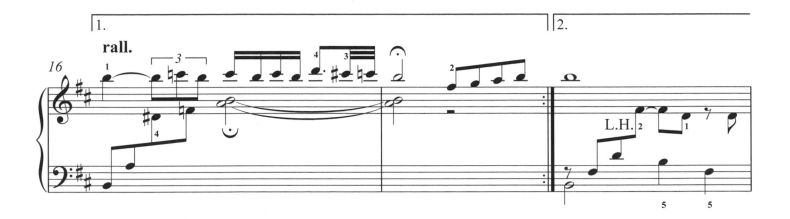

Blue Velvet
(from 'Blue Velvet')

Words & Music by Bernie Wayne & Lee Morris

Gently ♩ = 80

Brokeback Mountain (Theme)
(from 'Brokeback Mountain')

Music by Gustavo Santoalalla

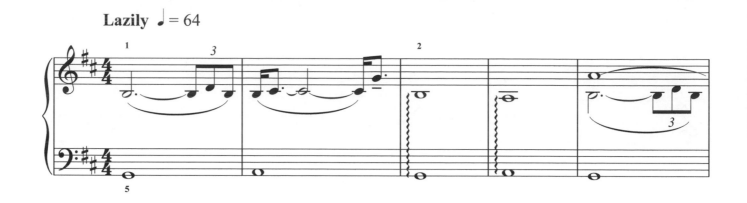

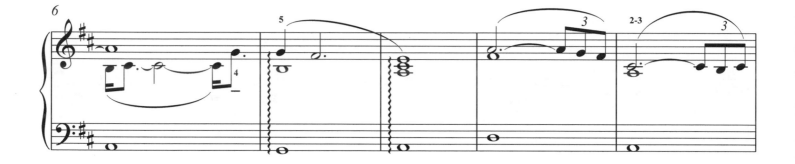

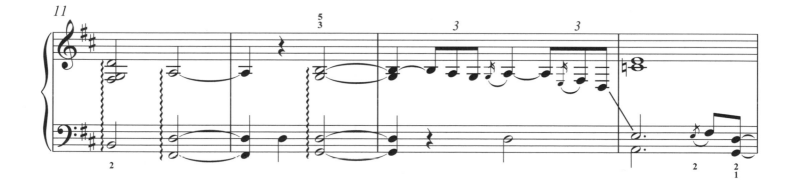

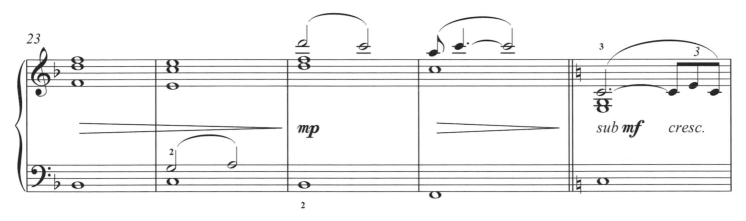

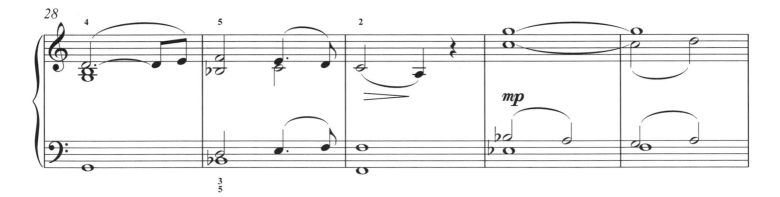

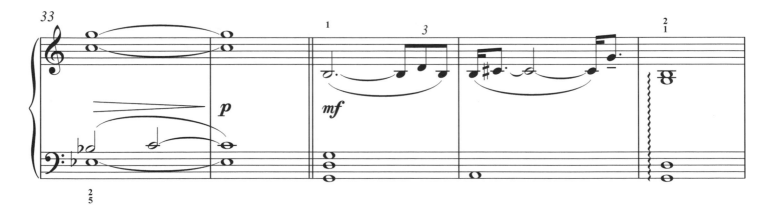

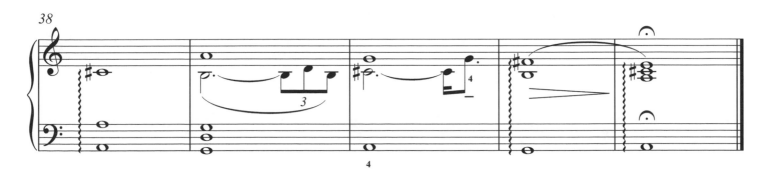

Circle Of Life
(from Walt Disney Pictures' 'The Lion King')

Words by Tim Rice & Music by Elton John

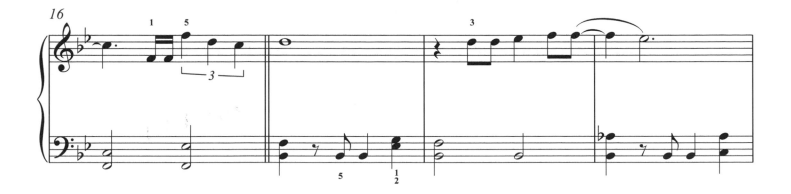

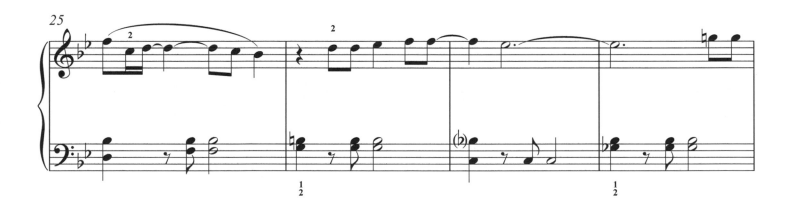

Clair De Lune
(from 'Ocean's 11')

Music by Claude Debussy

Dancing With The Bear
(from 'Finding Neverland')

Music by Jan A.P. Kaczmarek

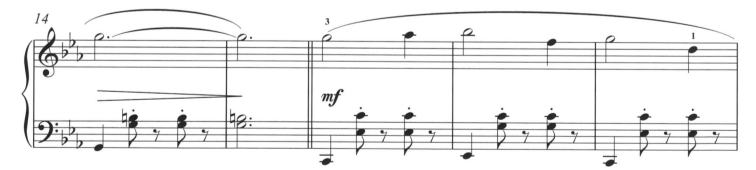

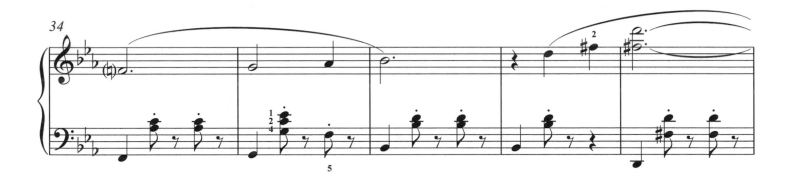

Eternal Vow
(from 'Crouching Tiger, Hidden Dragon')

Music by Tan Dun

Freely ♩ = 120

Eye Of The Tiger
(from 'Rocky III')

Words & Music by Jim Peterik & Frank Sullivan III

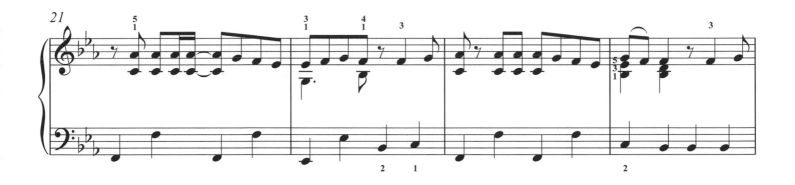

Funeral/Justin's Breakdown
(from 'The Constant Gardener')

Music by Alberto Iglesias

FUNERAL

Slowly and solemnly ♩ = 48

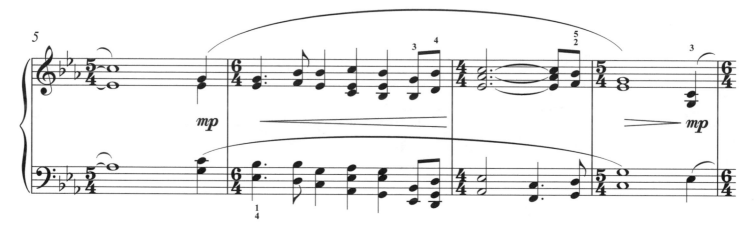

JUSTIN'S BREAKDOWN
Very slow and free

poco **f** *warm*

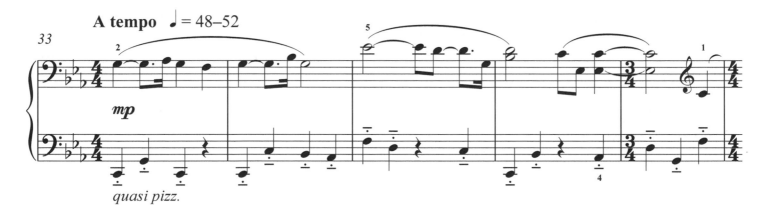

A tempo ♩ = 48–52

mp

quasi pizz.

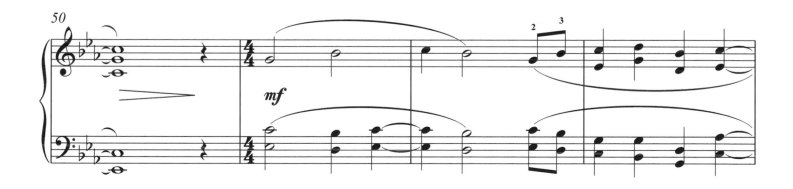

(I'm Your) Hoochie Coochie Man
(from 'Cadillac Records')

Words & Music by Willie Dixon

Allegro ♩ = 120

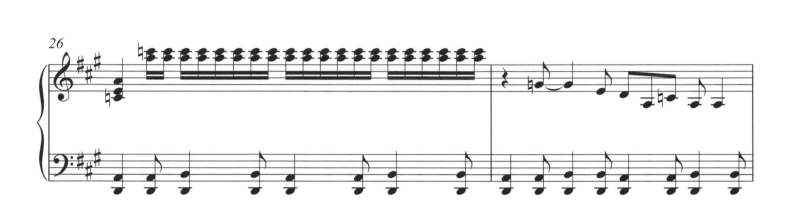

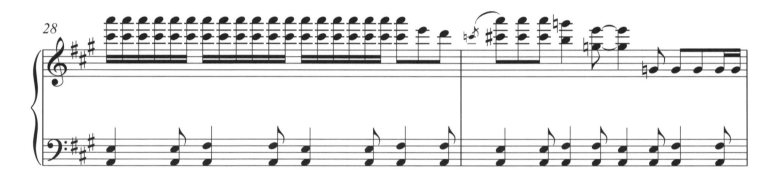

Georgia On My Mind
(from 'Ray')

Words by Stuart Gorrell & Music by Hoagy Carmichael

Moderately, with a blues feel

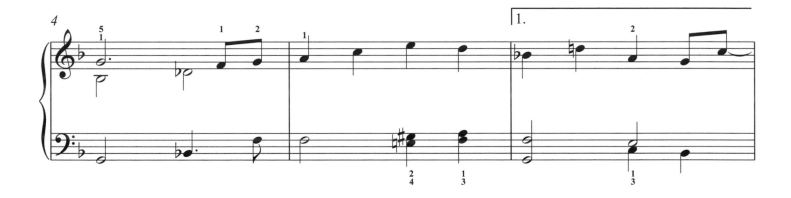

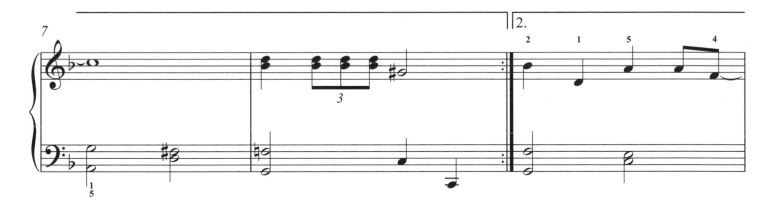

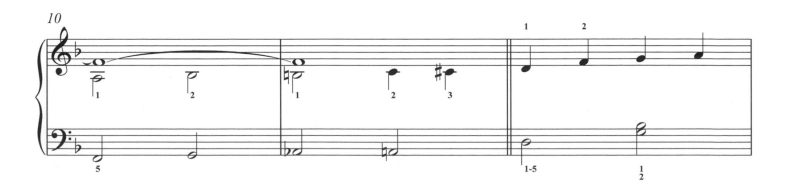

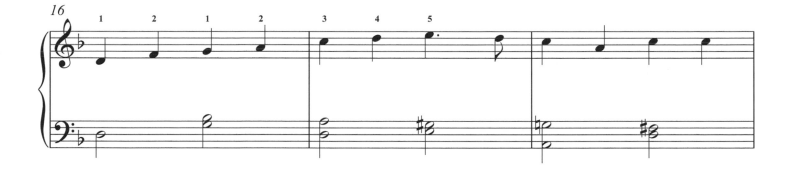

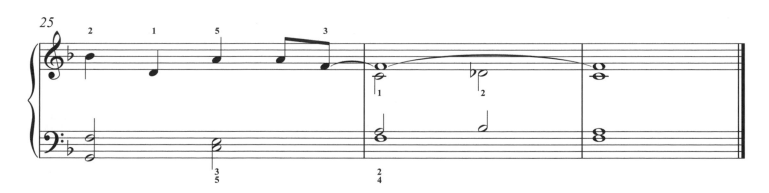

A Hard Day's Night
(from 'A Hard Day's Night')

Words & Music by John Lennon & Paul McCartney

Moderately

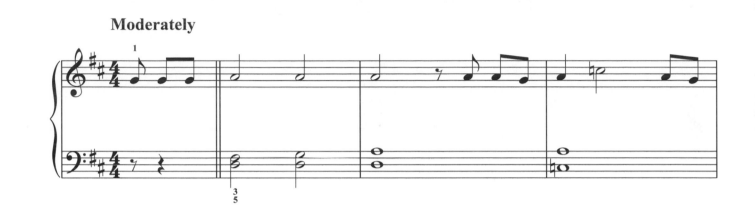

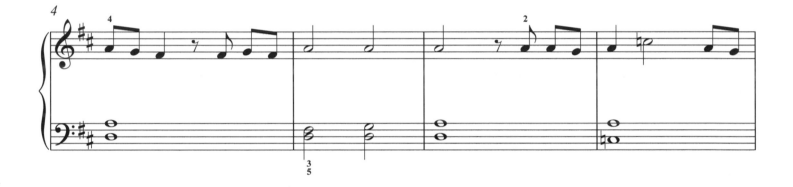

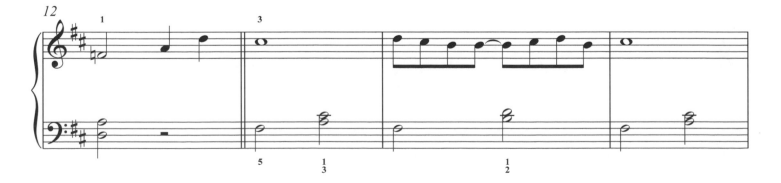

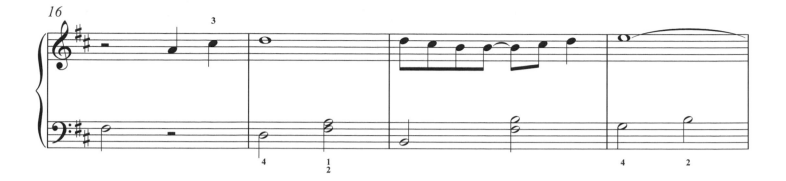

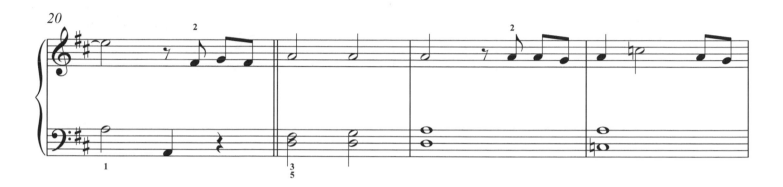

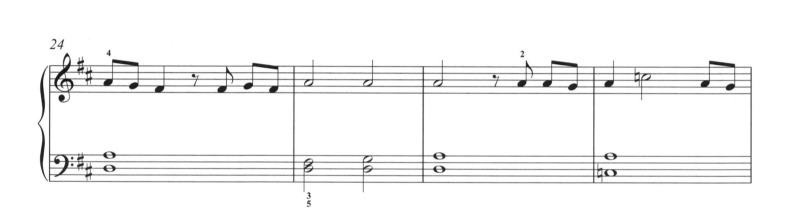

poco rit.

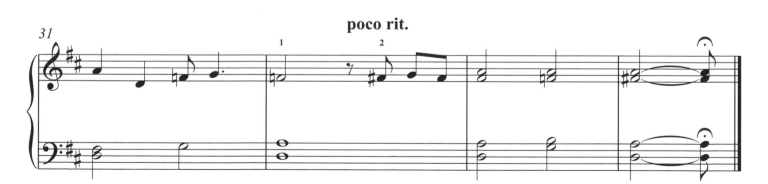

Honor Him/Now We Are Free
(from 'Gladiator')

Music by Hans Zimmer/Music by Hans Zimmer, Lisa Gerrard & Klaus Badelt

HONOR HIM

♩ = 66

poco accel.

♪ = ♩ = 140

NOW WE ARE FREE

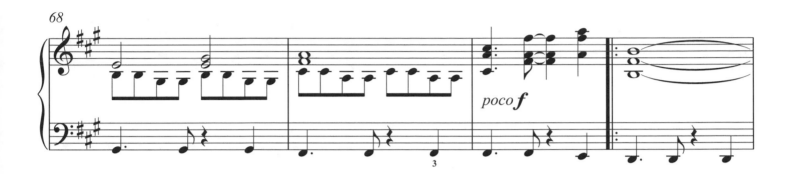

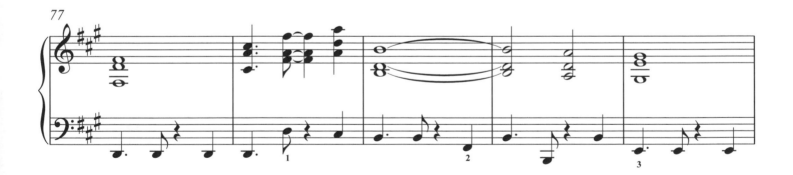

Slower, freely

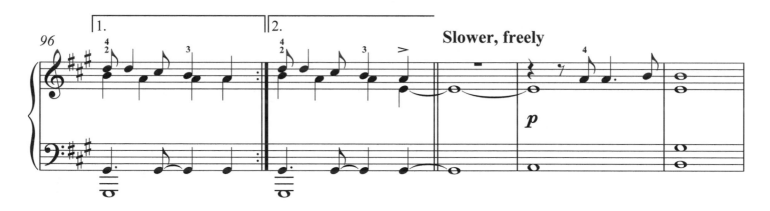

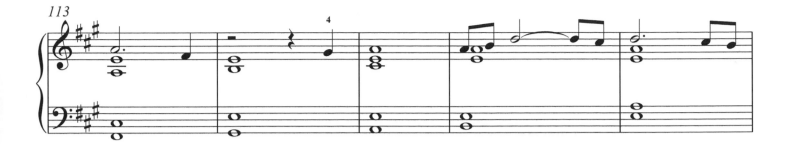

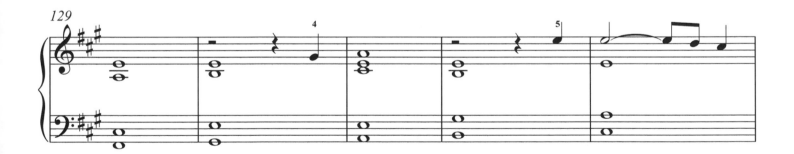

I Had A Farm In Africa
(Main Title from 'Out Of Africa')

Music by John Barry

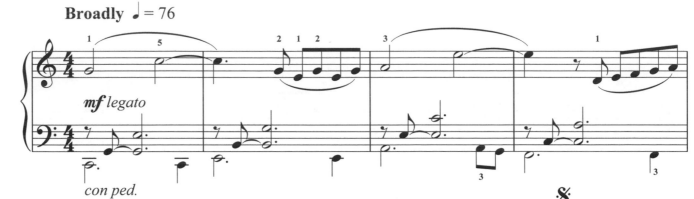

Into The West
(from 'The Lord Of The Rings: The Return Of The King')

Words & Music by Annie Lennox, Howard Shore & Fran Walsh

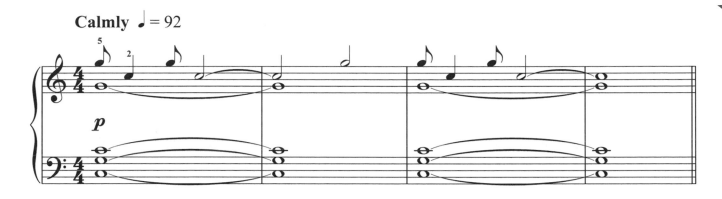

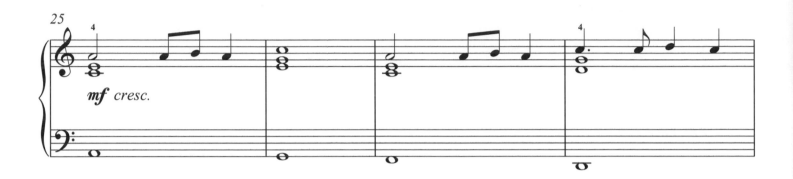

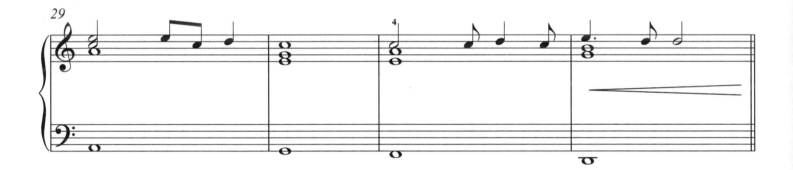

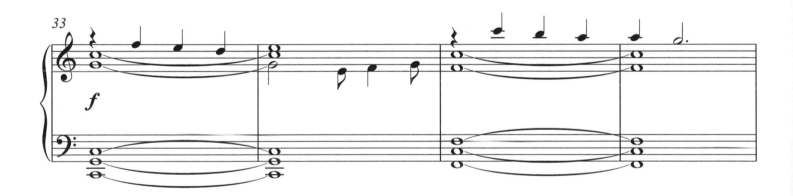

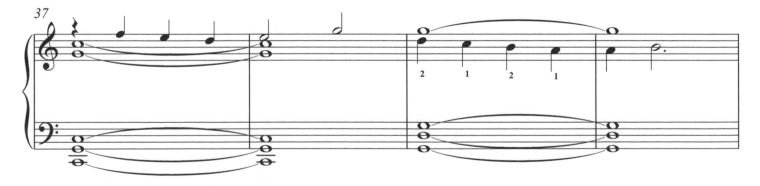

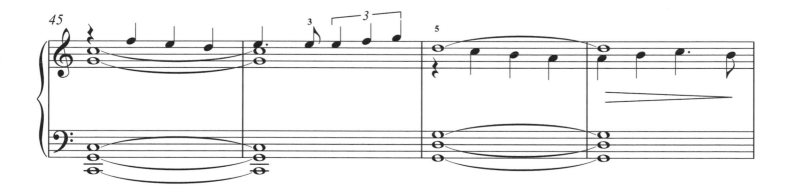

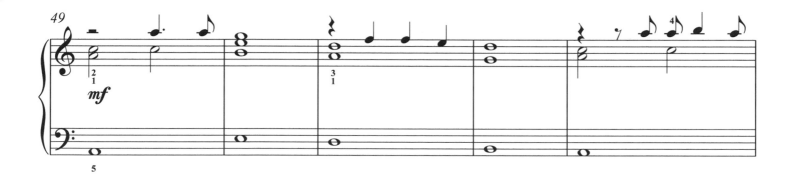

(I've Had) The Time Of My Life
(from 'Dirty Dancing')

Words & Music by Frankie Previte, John DeNicola & Donald Markowitz

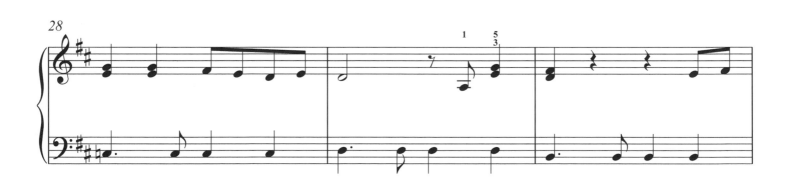

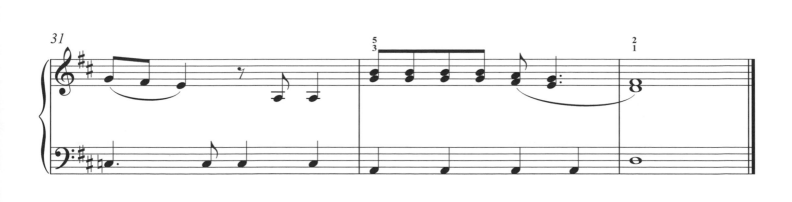

Le Banquet
(from 'Amélie')

Music by Yann Tiersen

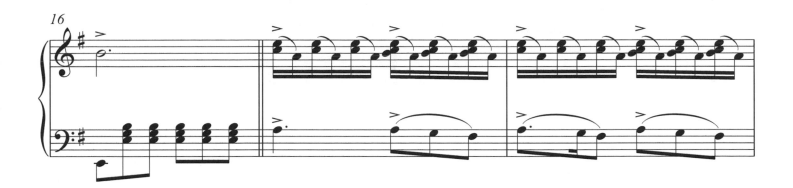

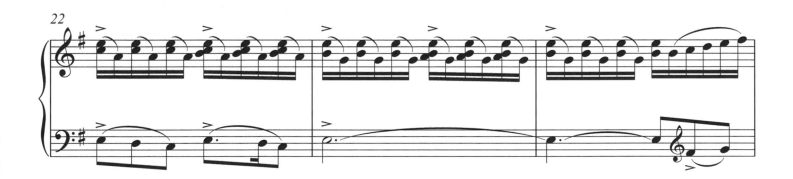

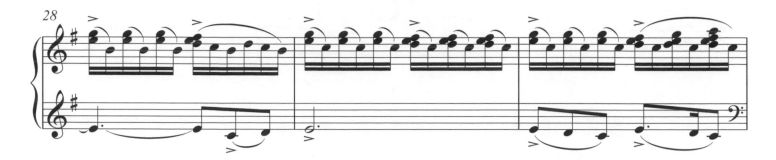

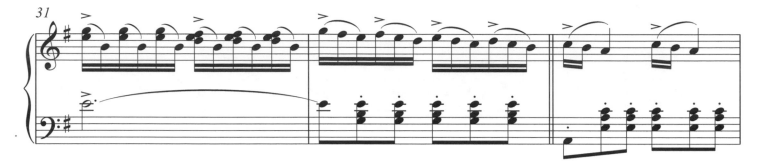

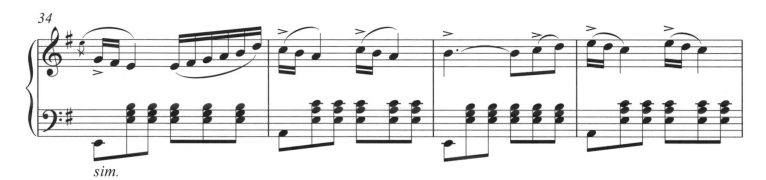

Live And Let Die
(from 'Live And Let Die')

Words & Music by Paul & Linda McCartney

Lawrence Of Arabia (Main Titles)
(from 'Lawrence Of Arabia')

Music by Maurice Jarre

Slowly, with expression

A Man And A Woman
(from 'Un Homme et une Femme')

Words by Pierre Barouh & Music by Francis Lai. English Translation by Jerry Keller

Moderately

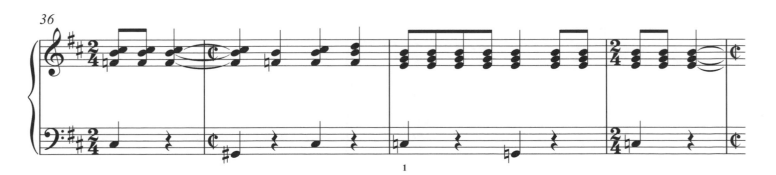

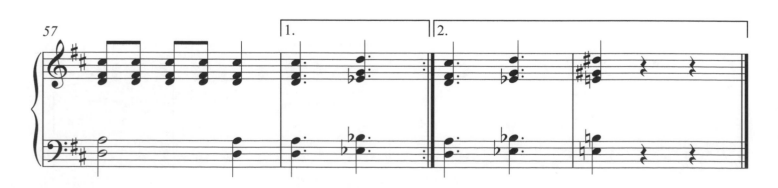

Mothersbaugh's Canon
(from 'The Royal Tenenbaums')

Music by Mark Mothersbaugh

Slowly and thoughtfully ♩ = 63

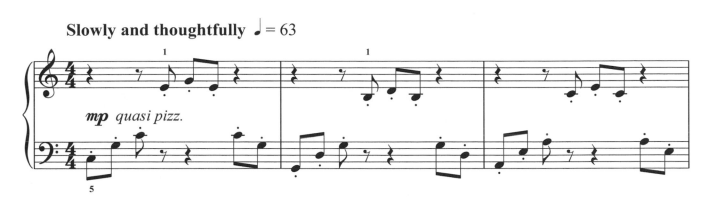

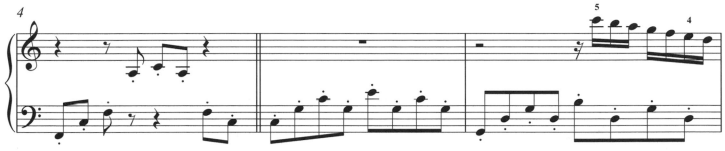

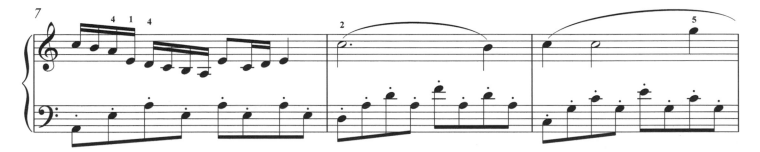

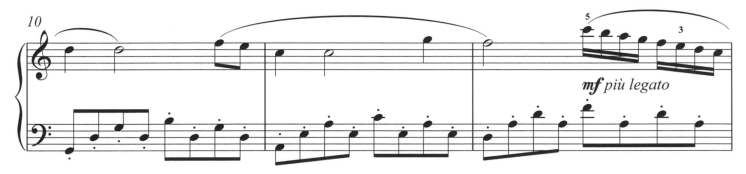

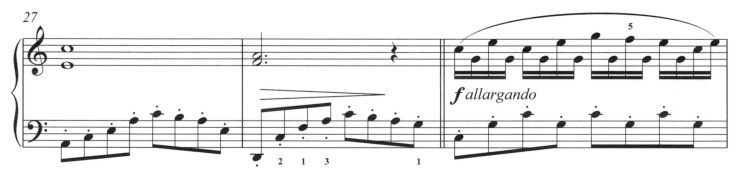

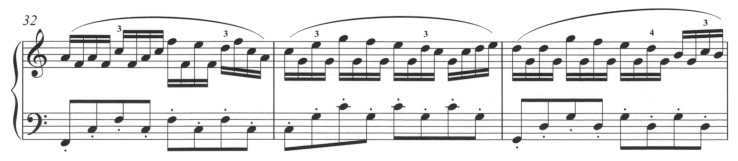

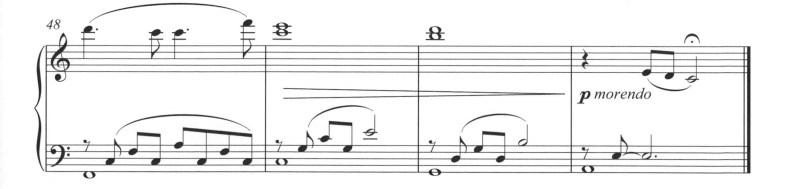

Nothing's Gonna Stop Us Now
(from 'Mannequin')

Words & Music by Diane Warren & Albert Hammond

Moderate rock

D.S. al Coda

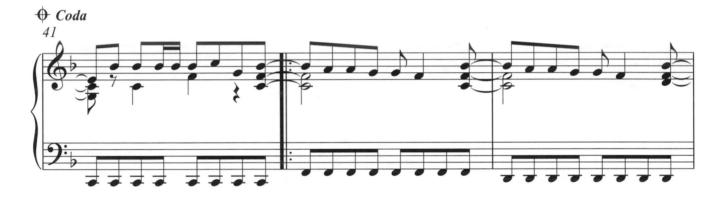

⊕ *Coda*

Repeat and fade ad lib.

Oh, Pretty Woman
(from 'Pretty Woman')

Words & Music by Roy Orbison & Bill Dees

Once Upon A Time In The West
(from 'Once Upon A Time In The West')

Music by Ennio Morricone

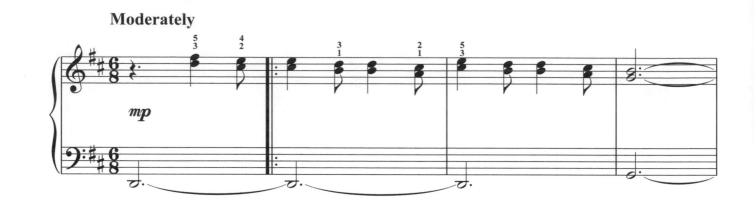

Passage Of Time
(from The Miramax Motion Picture 'Chocolat')

Music by Rachel Portman

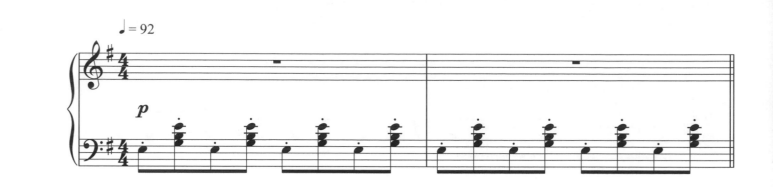

Poco più mosso

Pelagia's Song
(from 'Captain Corelli's Mandolin')

Music by Stephen Warbeck

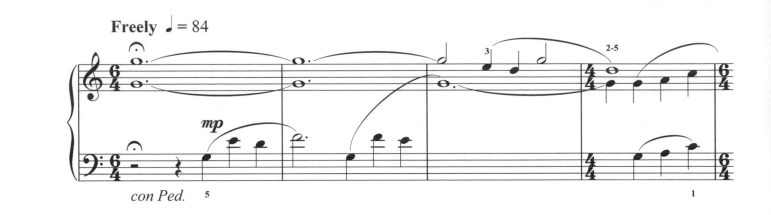

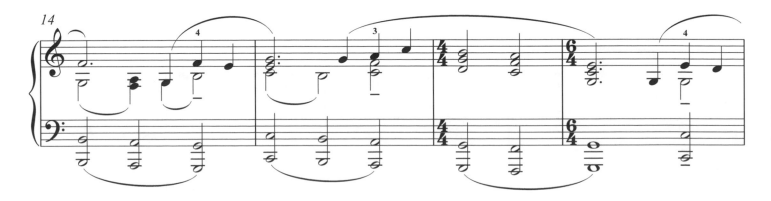

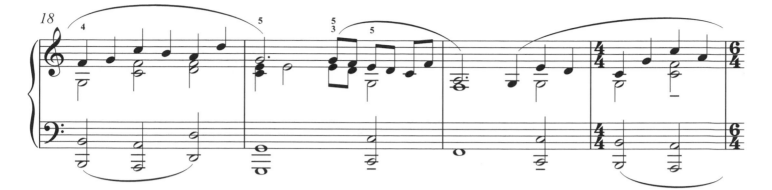

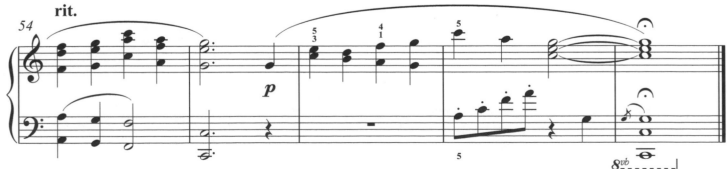

Pelle Erobreren
(from 'Pelle The Conqueror')

Music by Stefan Nilsson

Expressively ♩ = 53

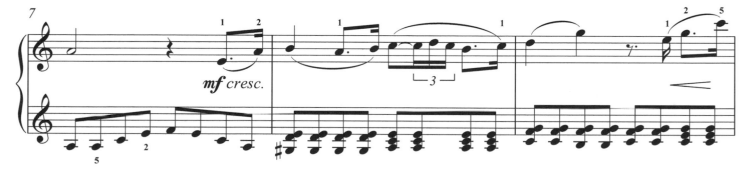

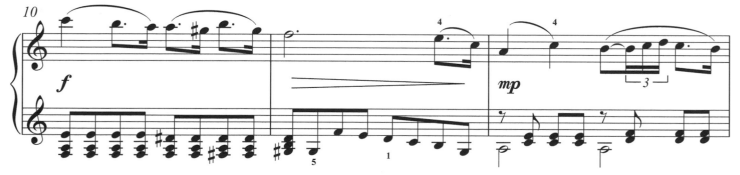

PM's Love Theme
(from 'Love Actually')

Words & Music by Craig Armstrong

Prologue: My Life Before Me
(from 'The Portrait Of A Lady')

Music by Wojciech Kilar

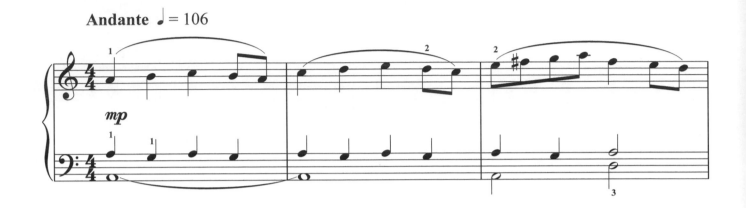

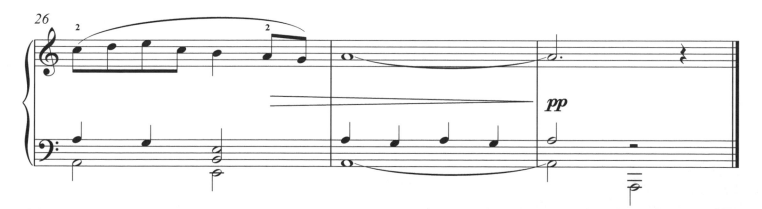

The Promise
(from 'The Piano')

Music by Michael Nyman

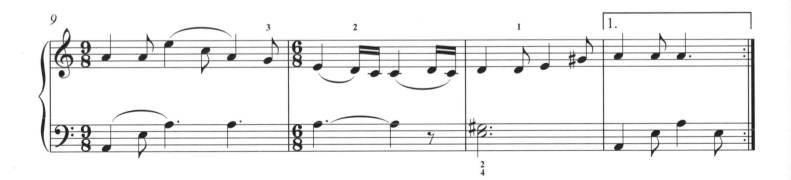

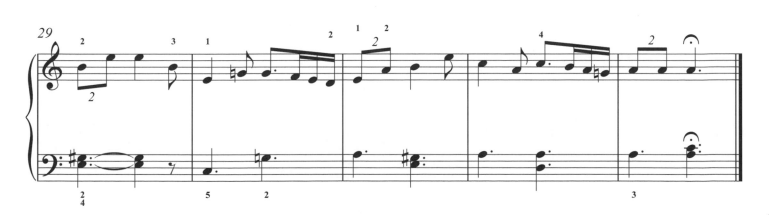

Reprise...
(from 'Spirited Away')

Music by Joe Hisaishi

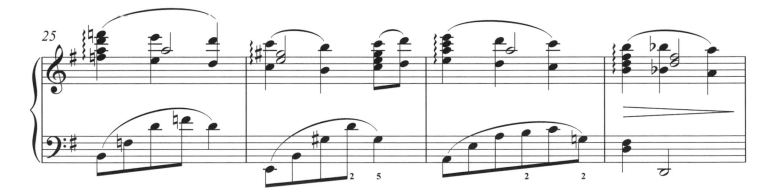

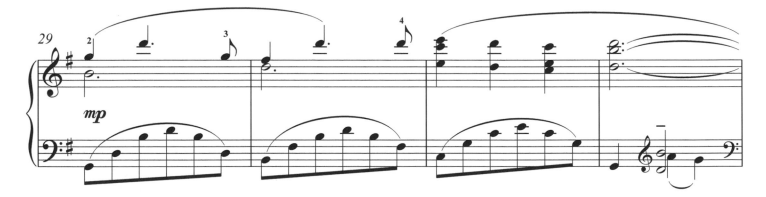

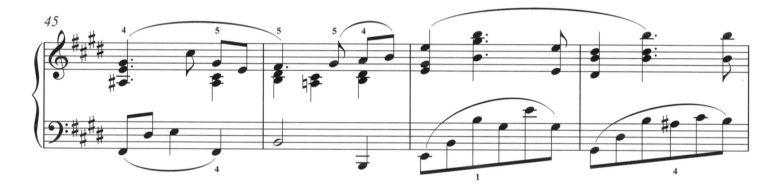

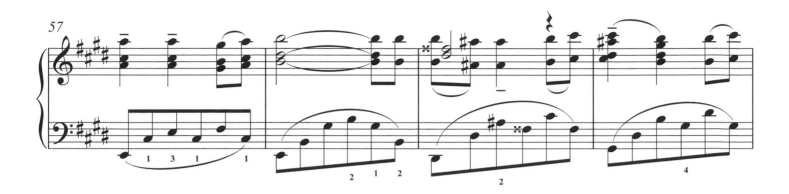

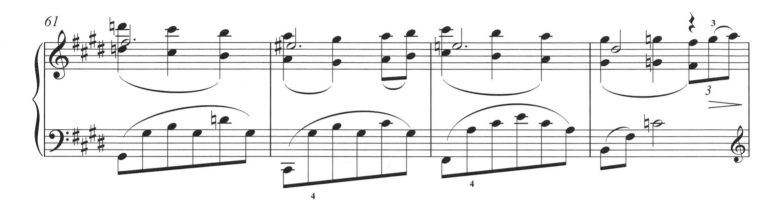

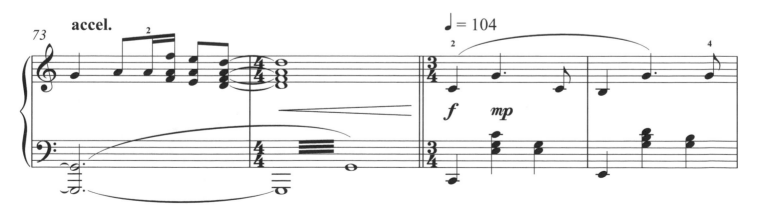

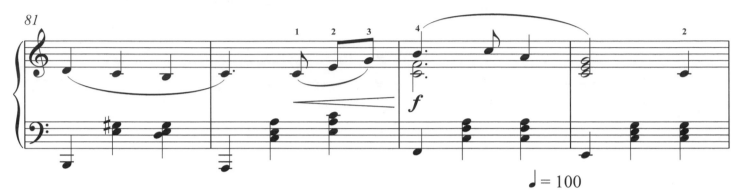

poco rall.

♩ = 100

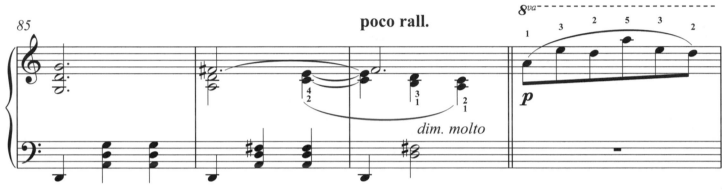

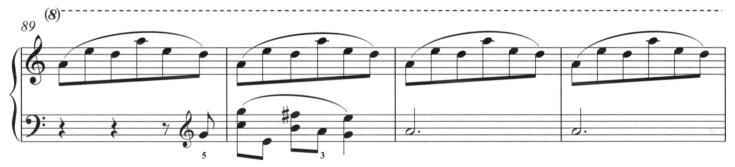

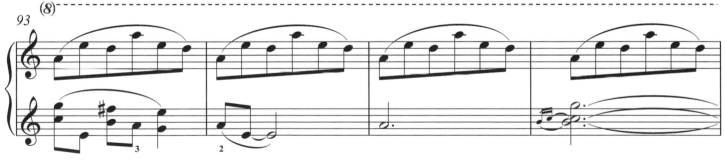

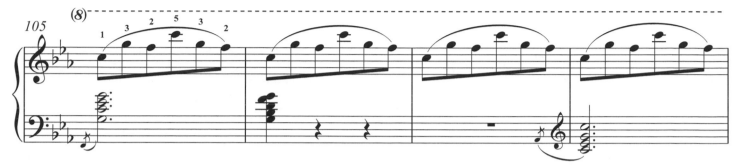

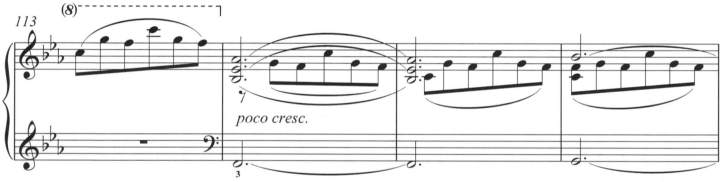

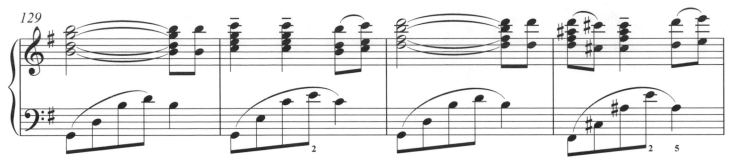

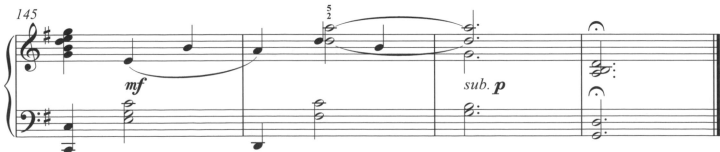

Rosie Darko
(from 'Donnie Darko')

Music by Michael Andrews

Più mosso

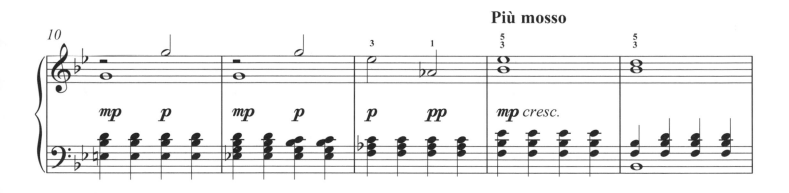

rall.

Road To Perdition
(from 'Road To Perdition')

Music by Thomas Newman

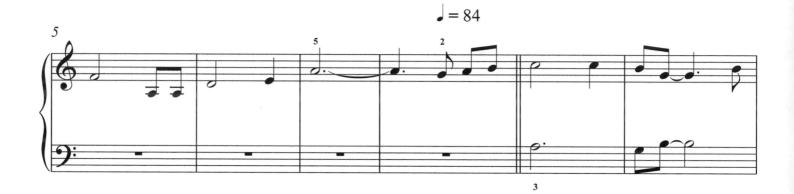

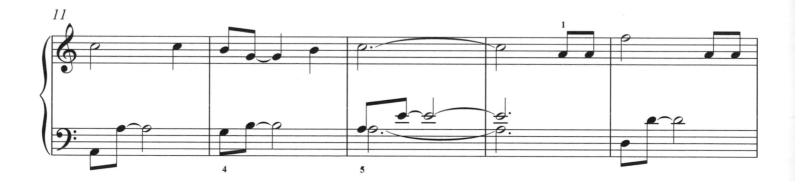

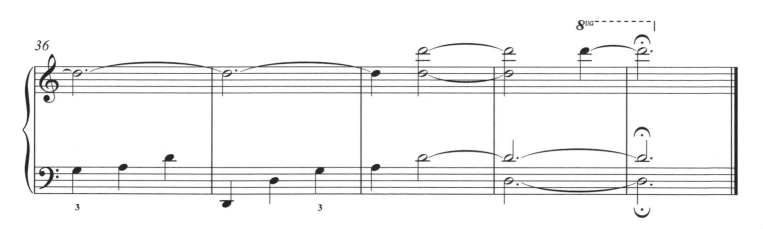

Rule The World
(from 'Stardust')

Words & Music by Mark Owen, Gary Barlow, Jason Orange & Howard Donald

Steadily ♩ = 82

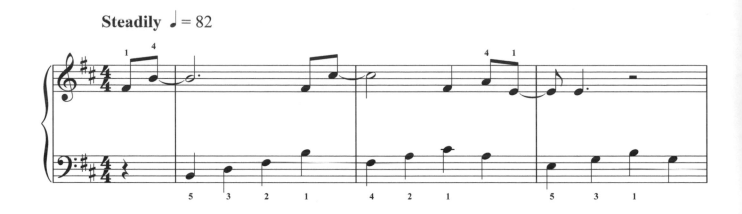

Scene D'Amour
(from 'Vertigo')

Music by Bernard Herrmann

Moderately with expression

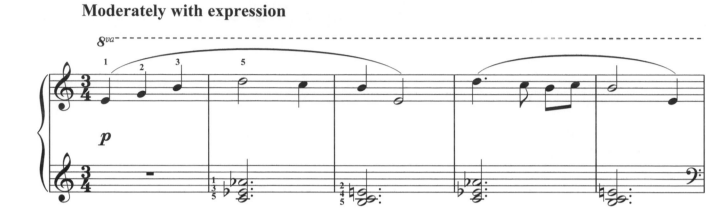

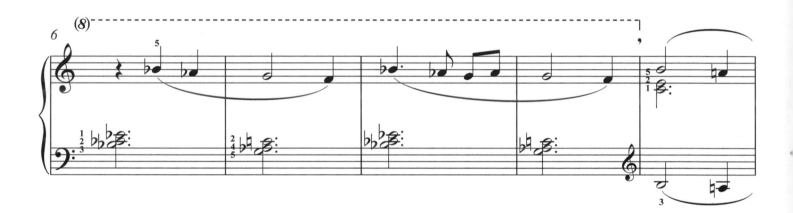

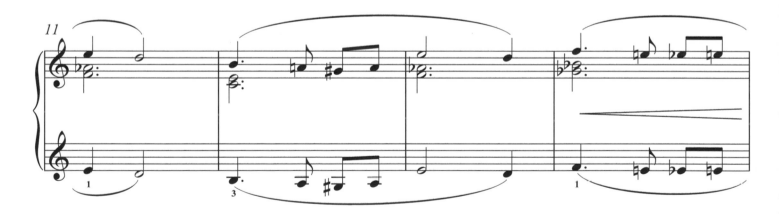

102

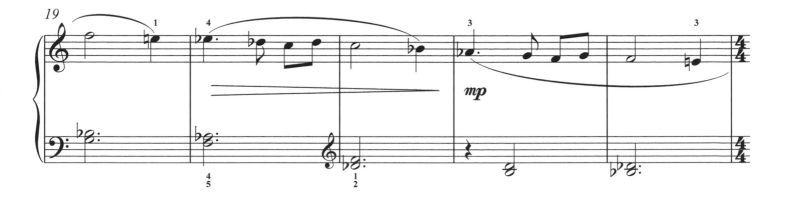

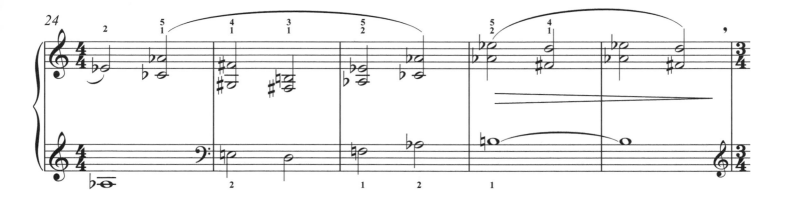

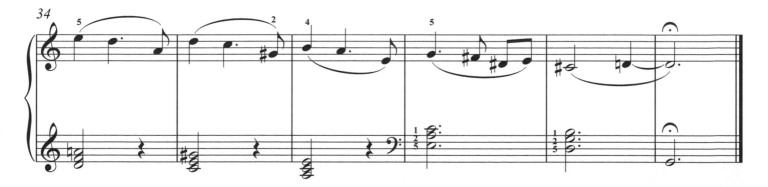

The Shower
(from 'Dressed To Kill')

Music by Pino Donaggio

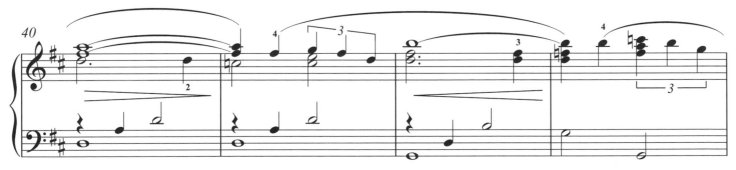

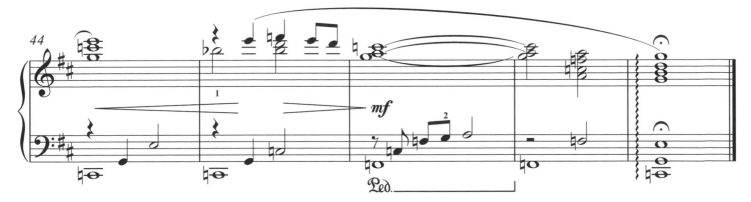

The Sound Of Silence
(from 'The Graduate')

Words & Music by Paul Simon

Moderato ♩ = 100

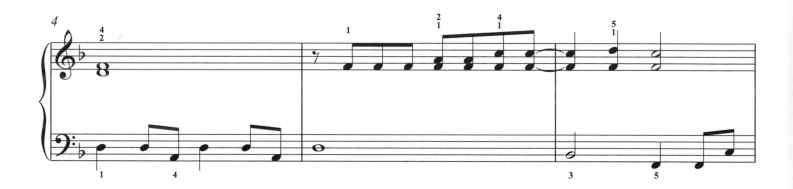

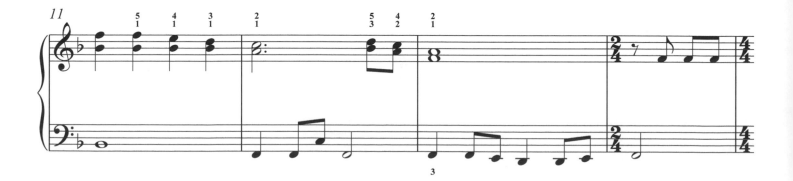

106

St. Vitus' Dance
(from 'A Knight's Tale')

Words & Music by Carter Burwell

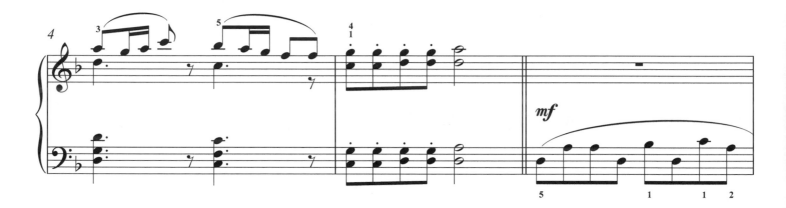

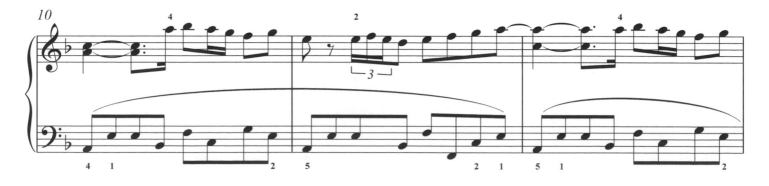

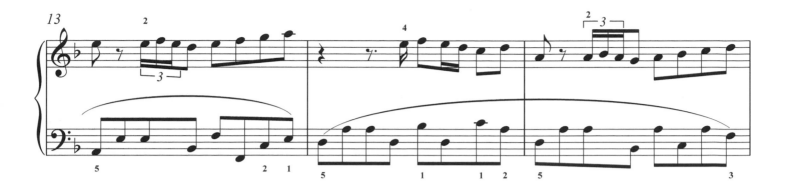

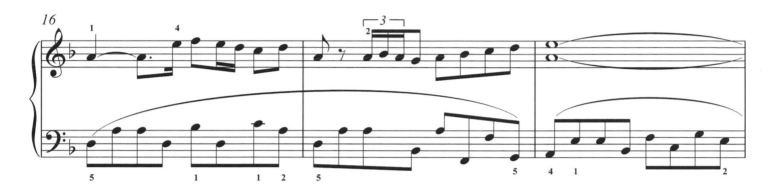

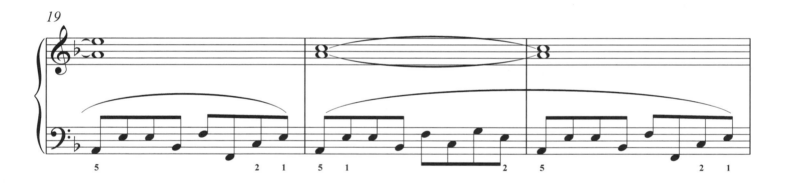

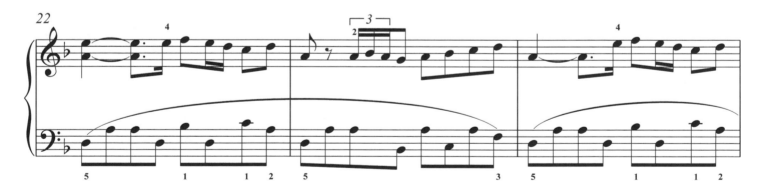

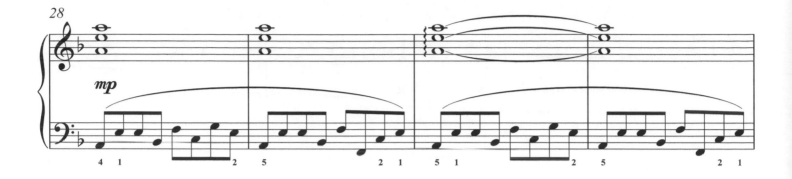

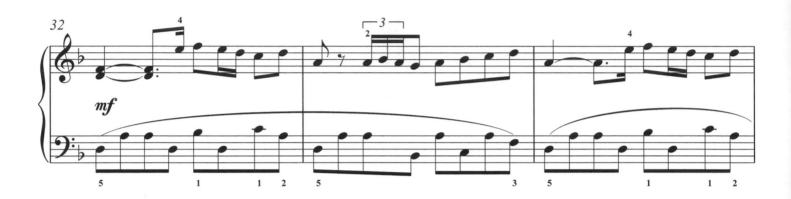

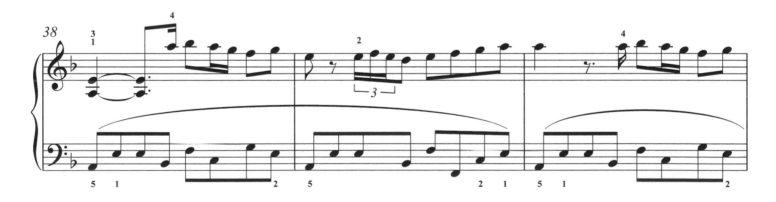

You Know My Name
(Theme from 'James Bond: Casino Royale')

Words & Music by David Arnold & Chris Cornell

Heavy Rock ♩ = 136

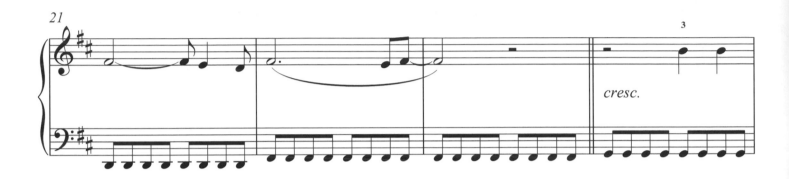

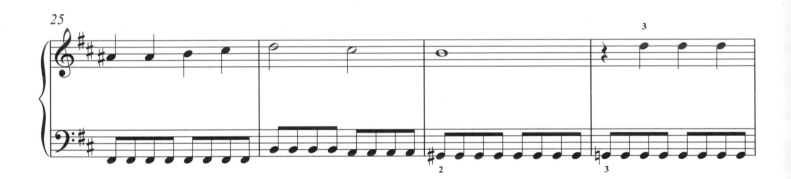

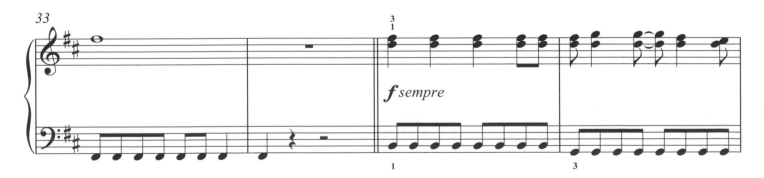

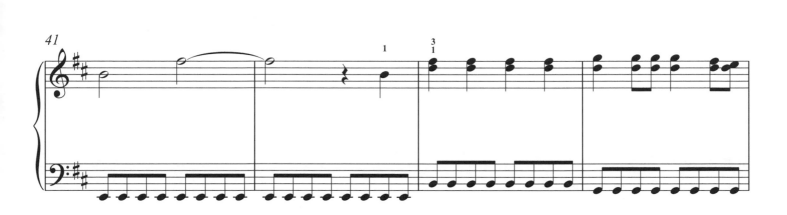

Sweets To The Sweet—Farewell
(from 'Hamlet')

Music by Patrick Doyle

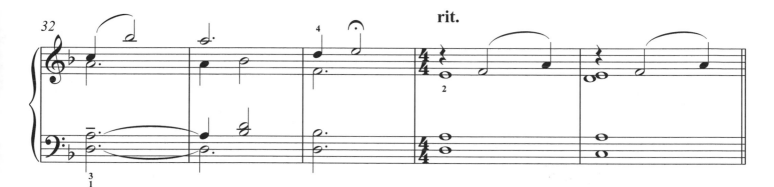

rit.

A tempo ♩ = 80

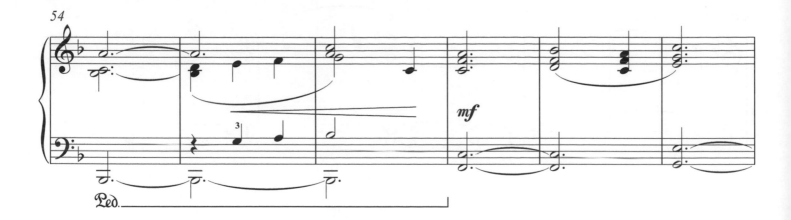

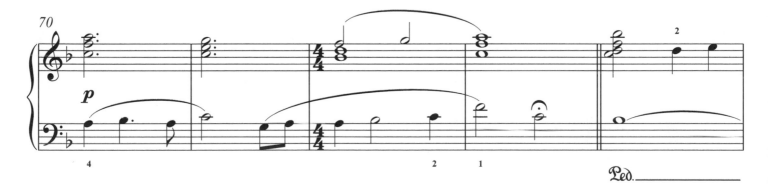

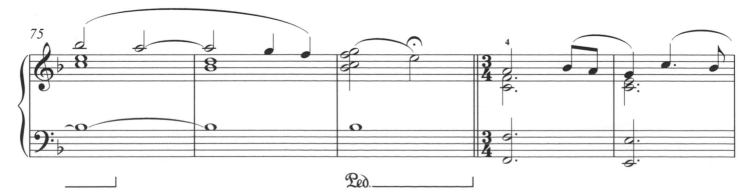

Up Where We Belong
(from 'An Officer And A Gentleman')

Words & Music by Jack Nitzsche, Will Jennings & Buffy Sainte-Marie

Voulez-Vous
(from 'Mamma Mia!')

Words & Music by Benny Andersson & Björn Ulvaeus

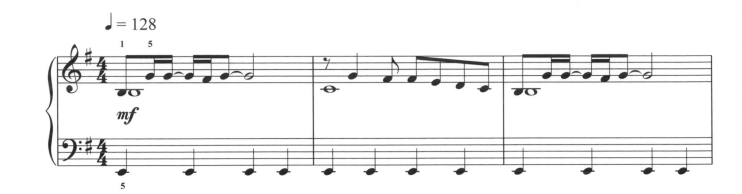

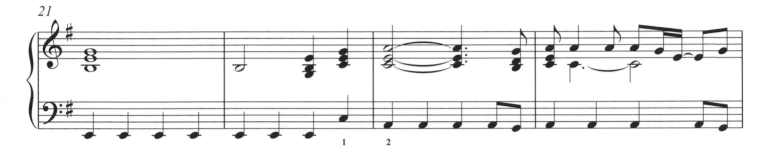

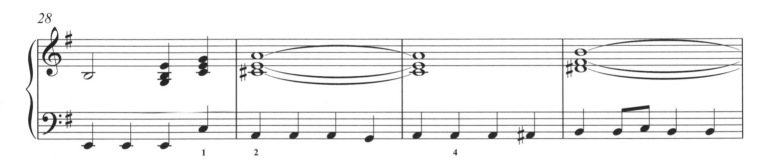

A Whole New World
(from 'Aladdin')

Words by Tim Rice & Music by Alan Menken

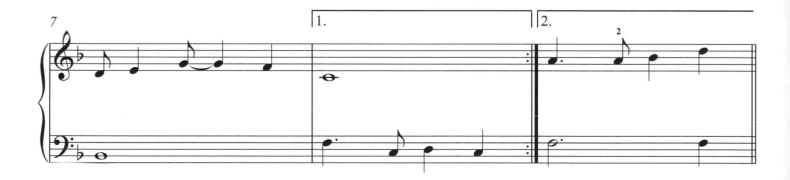

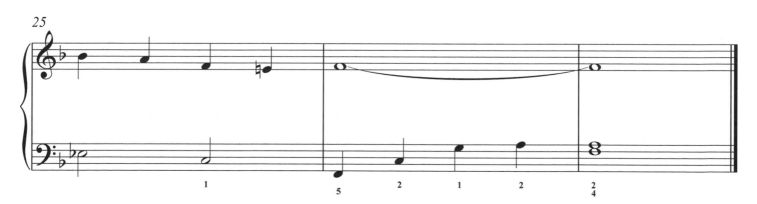

Will And Elizabeth

(from 'Pirates Of The Caribbean: The Curse Of The Black Pearl')

Music by Klaus Badelt

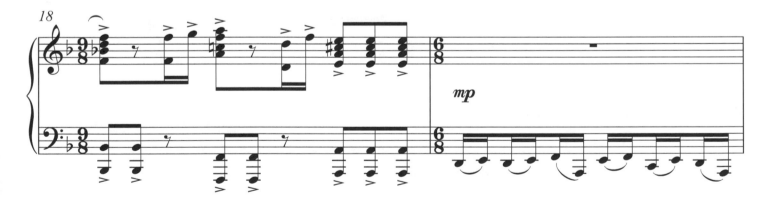

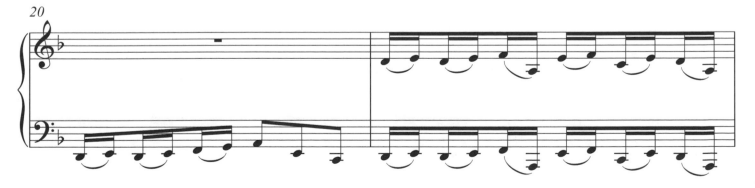

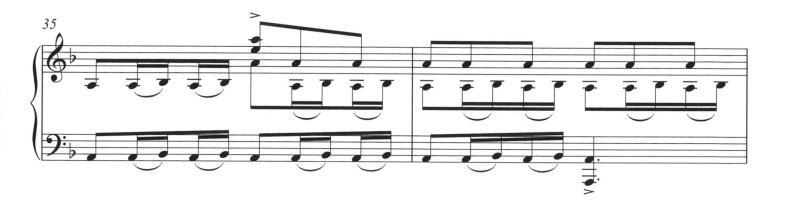